HAL•LEONARD®
TRUMPET PLAY-ALONG

AUDIO
ACCESS
INCLUDED

VOL. 2

TRUMPET CLASSICS

T0070829

CONTENTS

To access audio visit:
www.halleonard.com/mylibrary

Enter Code
5880-6044-6434-5562

ISBN 978-1-4950-0012-6

Visit Hal Leonard Online at
www.halleonard.com

HAL•LEONARD®
CORPORATION

7777 W. BLUEMOUND RD. P.O. BOX 13819
MILWAUKEE, WISCONSIN 53213

Ciribiribin

Based on the original melody by A. Pestalozza

English Version by Harry James, Jack Lawrence, Patti Andrews, Maxene Andrews and Laverne Andrews

Feels So Good

By Chuck Mangione

Java

By Marilyn Schack, Freddy Friday, Allen Toussaint and Alvin Tyler

Music To Watch Girls By

By Sid Ramin

Spanish Flea

Words and Music by Julius Wechter

Sugar Blues

Words by Lucy Fletcher
Music by Clarence Williams

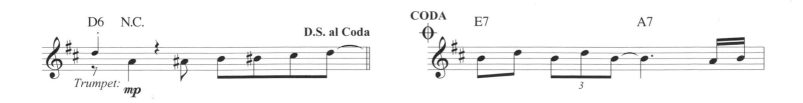

The Toy Trumpet

By Raymond Scott

A Taste of Honey

Words by Ric Marlow
Music by Bobby Scott

HAL·LEONARD®
TRUMPET PLAY-ALONG

The Trumpet Play-Along Series will help you play your favorite songs quickly and easily. Just follow the printed music, listen to the sound-alike recordings and hear how the trumpet should sound, and then play along using the separate backing tracks.

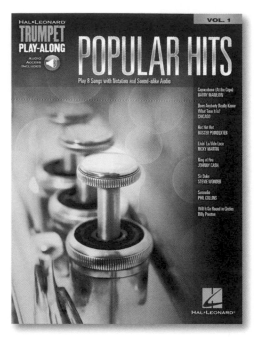

1. POPULAR HITS
Copacabana (At the Copa) (Barry Manilow) • Does Anybody Really Know What Time It Is? (Chicago) • Hot Hot Hot (Buster Poindexter) • Livin' La Vida Loca (Ricky Martin) • Ring of Fire (Johnny Cash) • Sir Duke (Stevie Wonder) • Sussudio (Phil Collins) • Will It Go Round in Circles (Billy Preston).

00137383
Book/Online Audio
$16.99

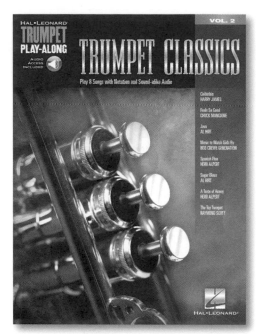

2. TRUMPET CLASSICS
Ciribiribin (Harry James) • Feels So Good (Chuck Mangione) • Java (Al Hirt) • Music to Watch Girls By (Bob Crewe Generation) • Spanish Flea (Herb Alpert) • Sugar Blues (Al Hirt) • A Taste of Honey (Herb Alpert) • The Toy Trumpet (Raymond Scott).

00137384
Book/Online Audio
$16.99

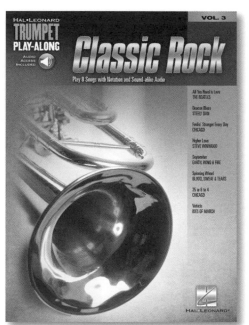

3. CLASSIC ROCK
All You Need Is Love (The Beatles) • Deacon Blues (Steely Dan) • Feelin' Stronger Every Day (Chicago) • Higher Love (Steve Winwood) • September (Earth, Wind & Fire) • Spinning Wheel (Blood, Sweat & Tears) • 25 or 6 to 4 (Chicago) • Vehicle (Ides of March).

00137385
Book/Online Audio
$16.99

4. GREAT THEMES
Cherry Pink and Apple Blossom White (Perez Prado) • Deborah's Theme (Ennio Morricone) • Dragnet (Walter Schumann) • The Godfather Waltz (Nino Rota) • Gonna Fly Now (Bill Conti) • Green Hornet Theme (Al Hirt) • The Odd Couple (Neal Hefti) • Sugar Lips (Al Hirt).

00137386
Book/Online Audio
$16.99

HAL·LEONARD®
CORPORATION
7777 W. BLUEMOUND RD. P.O. BOX 13819 MILWAUKEE, WI 53213